to the strange and wandering:

within you, there are
worlds to be explored.
find your worth.
find your heart
find your soul.
discover yourself,
over and over again.

-z.k.d

MORE SOUL THAN HUMAN

Poetry & Prose
By: Zachry K. Douglas

the broken will always

be able to love harder

than most. once you

have been in the dark,

you learn to appreciate

everything that shines.

i know it feels like you have more time than you know what to do with. as much as you want to believe in that scenario, it is the furthest thing from the truth.
the reality in which you are existing in, is a false sense of meaning for those who believe there is always more time.

learn how to catch the moments. learn how to unfold them in ways you see fit. learn how to hold your breath and breathe out of your soul.

do not kill off who you are so someone else can use what you have. do not hand yourself out so freely.

be selfish with your own life.
i promise you, it's okay.

you are the strongest woman i know. you are the bravest woman who has ever ventured into my life. you are where you're supposed to be and no matter what comes in front of us, we will handle it together, because we are us. no matter what it is, i will back you one hundred percent and stand in front of you when i need to and stand behind you when you feel like falling back into me to hold you up. you are my soul's best friend. i love you with every fiber of my being. we will get through anything together because we are each other's reflection, and in this life, the ones we are living now, there is and will always be an us. i love you. i love you. i love you. i'm sorry you're going through the things you are, sweetheart, but you're my baby, and i will be here for you. deep breaths, and feel me kissing your lips. feel my arms around you. feel my energy. feel my hands holding yours. you got this. we got this.

i remember them saying, "what do you want to be when you get older?" i never knew what i wanted to be when i was young. i remember the thought of flying planes or being a fireman was something that intrigued me. but i think there are common answers to that question and i was never a common kid. people always told me that i needed to know so i could pursue something and make life more meaningful. but does it really mean more if you do know? all i wanted to do was simply matter to someone that cared for me, and in return, give them a type of love they never knew they could hold in their heart forever. i once had a few rich friends that never needed to worry about the next day. i've also met a lot of people on busy street corners that are living with a smile no matter what is going on around them. happiness is something we are all born with. it is up to us to grow it and spread it to the edges of the universe. do not be common. stretch your mind around new ideas and just fucking live. smile at strangers. laugh with family and friends as often as you can. learn how to enjoy a life where waking up and getting out of bed actually means something to you. strive to be different. this world is already full of normal.

it's about finding souls
who vibe with yours.
who love like yours.
who laughs like the sun
and moon are watching
and are in love with
everything they see.

<be one of them>

open your heart to the universe and in return, you will see a soul. one that was sheltered well beyond the walls and screams. one that was abandoned, but found refuge in the sounds of nothing. one that couldn't argue with anyone, because the energy used could never be returned. one that love often played with, but never gave completely. one that sleeps with a memory based off of movies and how books typically end without a true ending. one that consistently finds an altar of stars beneath his knees when the world above him becomes a roof he no longer needs.

show yourself to the stars and you will become the wild you have underneath your fingernails. the time you tried to hold onto the planet so you wouldn't fall off. you must not be scared of the gravity. it is only here for our imagination to stay with us.

we come into this world

in hopes of finding someone

who loves to sit and stay up

with our weird and crazy soul.

there's a place where chaos
changes the eyes and tickles
the fire inside of our hearts.

                      <i hope you get there>
                      <i hope it finds you first>

don't let the world get under your skin.
open your chest and feel everything instead.
life becomes increasingly more in our favor
once we regulate what goes and who stays
for the lifetime coming our way.

he was her hero. the soldier of her soul
that fought to keep each beat of her heart
alive just so she could be saved. she was his
hero. the queen of his heart and the very
reason it continued to play the sounds of his
soul. she fought like hell because that's what
angels do.

        written with renee chandler.
              rest in paradise, sweet soul.
                      fuck cancer.

for the first time, i value my life, because you are a part of it. with you here, winter is finally defrosting from the bones it had been resting on. the birds are coming out of my eyes and ears. there are whispers amongst the wildlife that love has arrived, and is staying.

we are more than what our demons tell us we are. they are only alive if you allow them to be. love past their efforts. make it a promise to yourself. you deserve to be free.

there's a road only a few have the stomach for.
where digesting stars becomes the dream and
we live amongst the universe, unafraid of
what's hiding anymore.

before jumping into the water, make sure you can trust your feet to kick and your arms to move forward. we go as far as our ability to release our fear and embrace the uncertainty it projects. all life really is, is a lesson on survival.

i imagine a life where souls dance
and stomp their feet to the rhythm
of a thousand heartbeats. carelessly
falling in love with another soul,
just to feel alive. a place so divine,
no human is allowed inside.

i feel like i was not made for this place. maybe the universe made a universal mistake. my soul is too old for these young humans and their childish games.

<the many faults of a human>

when i close my eyes to kiss you, it is more than just to feel
your lips. i close them to see your soul. i close them to see
you. i close them to feel you. for when i close my eyes,
you are in front of the darkness. you become the light
i have been without since the sun gave me my name.

for a minute, she thought she was the moon with all of these juvenile wolves howling at her. while in reality, she was my universe; collecting my kisses and creating constellations on my heart for my soul to look at.

tucked away in the corner of my mind is where you will stay. you will forever be there; making love with my thoughts and sleeping soundly with my dreams.

i finally found someone as mad as me and she is everything that chaos has dreamt about.

for she stirred my soul with her soulful hands and now we are creating priceless art for the stars to look at.

i kissed the moon goodnight and she felt it from a world away. chills went out into the stars as the warmth from every planet and inch of space collected our dreams and brought them down to earth. that night, the sky was empty and i had never felt more love than giving all i could to someone who should never be without it.

all she wanted was to feel human again, so he grasped her hand and placed it over his heart, telling her, "this will beat for you until the end."

i once lit my soul on fire
with the tip of your tongue.
now the universe eternally
burns for only your love.

as they say, "there will always be more fish in the sea."
but to me, you were my catch. i wanted to be selfish
and keep you all to myself. now i know that i had to
let you go, for you needed the oceans. they will always
be your home and i took you away from a life you loved.
and for that, i am truly sorry, my dear.

you make me feel like i can
never get close enough to you.
as if our souls were trying to
hold each other, but our
bodies got in the way.

she was a rebel who was born with a fierce heart and a wild soul. i loved and respected her for both, but i did not want to confine her vibrant spirit in a fixated world. you see, she desired to be the actual bloom of life for those who were content with merely being alive. her smile set fire to the imagination of reality; ultimately becoming a trailblazer. and i, all i wanted to do was burn with her.

and if life should ever get in the way between you and i,
i will attach our memories to my heart, with just enough
string and fly it in the sky for you to always see.
wherever i go, you will forever be a part of me.

i like being alone.
crowds of people
drive my anxiety
through the roof.

my world. my reality.

i keep the company
that allows me to
stay grounded.

where souls find true love and the right heart in humans. where flesh only speaks to the flower and not the totality of life itself. there is no coming back from it if you make it. there is no other way to go than being with your soul's best friend and living a life where tomorrow is lived today, and only in a span of breaths given.

you ignorant fools,

all she ever wanted

was magic;

the kind she could finally believe in.

just because it might seem hopeless,

doesn't mean we should hope less.

you have never experienced

love until you have felt a

smile hold you in the

middle of the night.

if it were not for the mirror,
how would you see yourself?

would you even know where
to start? would you even care
if you couldn't?

i hope you can see, you.

my eyes are filled with memories of once before.
they speak for me when my mouth cannot find
the words. if you look deep enough you might
be able to see the curse; when they try and
close at night, they stay open to the universe.

it is not my first broken heart, nor will it be my last. i am good at being alone, but it is nice to hold someone's hand while the rest of the world sleeps. when for a moment in time i had the world next to me. she just didn't hold my hand, she held my soul, perfectly.

she said, "i give up. this damn world is too cold even for my warm heart." then her soul hugged her, and said, "not yet, love. there is more to life than worrying about what others keep inside. i need you to believe in me the same way i have always believed in you. keep fighting."

i told her to take my hand and show
me where it hurt the most. to my
astonishment, she took my hand
and placed it over my own
wounded heart.

with our love,
we kept the
world spinning;

allowing the stars a chance at immortality.

your name still echoes
through the cavities
of my lungs.

longing to cry out and
breathe you again.

all i ask is before you judge me, understand the scars that cover my heart. they tell a story of an intrepid soul who is trying to piece together a human with borrowed parts from the stars.

waking up, hungover on love, is a feeling i can never get enough of. when our fingertips touch, our souls begin to run away with each other to a place unknown to humans.

she turned to me, and said, "hold me." so i dropped the world i had been holding and picked her up with both hands. together we experienced what life is all about; understanding. love is not love until you have had your hands full of your own problems, only to realize that the universe you are living in was created by chaos.

where two souls cleanse themselves with each other's love.
where there is only love to give and love to understand.
where there is no walking out because the conversation
means talking it through and not leaving unbalanced.
where there is safety in only one person and not in a
multitude of numbers. where life asks to hold you
and you tell it how you want to be held.

                                                               <home>

the love i have lost is the kind that will never leave me. my life story was perfectly made from a beautiful tragedy. always remember why you cared and allow that passion to carry you through to your next journey. wherever that is, be happy that you are allowed another opportunity to live a life filled with tiny miracles every day.

your touch ignited all the stars in my soul.
creating a whole new universe of feelings
i have never known before.

i swear you could move
mountains with your
touch.

it is so powerful, i am
addicted to it, like a
soul jonesing for love.

for i am a poor man's soul
with the richest of hearts,
trying to survive in a world
where humans value wealth
more than they do love.

you are a special kind of human.
one that carries a soul that shines
for others.

one that becomes the brightest
when others think they have
been lost to the darkness.

one that is consumed by
rebuilding other broken
lighthouses along the
shore of life.

the true measure of a

human is not the size

of their heart, but how

well they comfort those

in need.

i will shape my spine
to fit in the contours
of your soul. i want to
experience what it is
like to forever live in
you. to forever kiss the
moon and become
something more than
just another face
refracting her light.

i have craved you ever since you made my soul speak of love. to have a single unmeasured moment with you, is all it will take to know i have been without everything that has given my lungs new magic to breathe.

always know this, darling.
my story will never be
more important than yours.
together, we will have the
universe giving us a standing
ovation, while it allows us to
have a sky full of stars all
to ourselves.

she was born with the light
of the moon inside her soul.

for it was just as bright and
beautiful as her natural glow.

for the rest of our lives,
we shall live as if death
will never be able to
find us or trick us
into believing this
is all there is, when
we both know how
much of a liar the
devil can be.

i once gave you the flower
of my soul to place in the
window of your heart.

to this day, it has continued
to grow with petals made of
memories that will never wilt
away.

<all it needs is the right amount of love>

when we touched,
we connected our
hearts with the stars;

providing a universal
night light for all of
those who had been
left alone and broken
in the dark.

in life, when you know
it is real, you will never
be able to hide love.

always remember that
every human has seen
it, but not every soul
has felt it.

she said she was broken
and love couldn't fix her,
so i showed her my heart
stitches and how love put
me back together.

i would literally give you
my spine if that could
finally make you stand
up for yourself.

there is nothing more cruel
than being made to believe
you can walk with your eyes
closed and still see what you
are told is out there.

i had this conversation with her
last night and asked how many
pillows she slept with. she said
none, then asked me the same
question.

"i sleep with one and keep another
one next to me. i've always kept an
extra pillow on that side.
just a habit i guess. sometimes, it's
nice to think someone is using it
to dream with me."

after it is all said and done.
when the moon has hung
herself because the sun
never came back up,
that is when i will stop
loving you. but not until
then. the sun will always
rise when i look into
your eyes.

it was our scars that brought you and
i together. they needed us to love each
other for them to finally heal.

never again shall we be afraid of what
others may say or think about our lives.
our story does not involve them, nor
will it ever make sense to those who fail
to understand that scars will always be
life written on flesh.

⟨they are simply words not everyone can read⟩

once my shadow became
my friend, i learned how
not to take life so seriously.
just because you might seem
odd to others, someone is
looking at you, thinking,

"maybe i'm not the only one who is alive."

i don't know what's going to happen. i guess that's just life for some of us. i could wake up tomorrow, get dressed and get in the jeep to drive somewhere random, then later that day, i could find someone, the one, who knows. i am not worried about finding love anymore. i've found you and whatever happens, i know i get to experience and share moments with a person that i never thought i would discover in this lifetime. time, place, and the spaces that make up reality has always been the most intriguing aspect of life for me. not knowing, yet knowing something great or horrible are the only two outcomes i know for sure that will greet us all one day, makes me appreciate everything i've been given and everything that has been taken away from me.

i could never be sure if it was the way her fingernails dug into my flesh, trying to find a better grip or the way she would lift her hips like the early morning fog, but she always drifted toward the ceiling every time i touched her and made her come along. she took my soul to places it had never been, and i hope to god i never have to leave her naked body ever again.

i have these dreams where i am walking amongst
old and broken tombstones and i arrive at one
that is inscribed with my name. it is where the
old me is buried. i take time to look around
the flowers that surround it and wonder who
put them there. i am not sure who else is in
this graveyard, but i awake right before i have
a chance to look around. my eyes fill up with
tears of remembrance, knowing just how bad
it was and how far i have come since putting
all of the bullshit and negativity behind me.
i hope i dream of that place again, so i can
finally lay the flowers i have in my hands
next to the words, "he lived a life where he
never worried about death. for he thought
it was just another word used by humans to
scare off the ability to find happiness."

all of my life i thought i could create happiness by just smiling at others and them smiling back at me. it's hard for me to sit here now and have this smile on my face when i wore a mask that hid the pain my soul was trying to show. i tried to bury it as deep as my bones could go, but now i know that the world needs to know how it feels to wear happiness. not just as a smile or showing your teeth because you think the universe needs to see them, but true happiness. the kind you wear every day, even when the pounding in your head overtakes your mind or when the stress and pressures from life fucking break you in half. judgment is inevitable. no matter who you think you are or portray yourself to be. once you learn that, the rain will feel different when you're trying to run inside to not get wet. you will not only want to dance in it, you will want to find the biggest puddle and announce to the world you aren't scared by doing the biggest cannonball. make a splash and create a chain reaction of hope for others to dance in.

i do not write or talk about death
that often, because i've seen and
felt too much of it to know you
will never be able to bring them
back to life. but i will always be
able to write and talk about
broken hearts, because if i write
and use enough ink from inside
of me, i might be able to restore
a few along my journey,
including my own that seems
to have been made with a fault
line at the at the seams of every
single bloody stitch i string together.

a kiss that completely sealed
all of my wounds. a touch
that repaired my hanging
heart. a look that connected
more than just eyes. it connected
our past lives. everything we have
touched in this earthly life, taught
us how direction only leads you so
far until you must trust yourself
and someone else to find your way
back home. a home that has yet been
built. a home that needed an other
pair of hands to place the pieces
together without the empty spaces.

i exposed my soul to the wonders of this
world. hoping i could locate where the
beginning and end meshed together to
form a future. only then did i understand
how it takes losing absolutely every fucking
thing you once owned to know greater
things await those who are willing to
shed not only their skin, but their bones
as well. we all must find that place where
our eyes turn into wanderers and our
minds find solace in the oceans and
trees surrounding our dreams,
but never keeping us enclosed.

i tried to pick a song out this morning
to play for you while you were sleeping,
but i could not find one that said your
name and how i want to hold your hand
while i kiss your neck. not a single one
could explain the love i have for you,
so i wrote this and left it on my pillow,
hoping these words will seep into your
dreams and wake you with that smile i
utterly adore.

the same mirror and reflection that once told me i am worthless and would never amount to anything, is no longer there. i now stand before it, screaming, "fuck you. i am worth everything you once tried to take from me." i am not just my own person anymore. i am individually secure, scars and all.

long before earth was created, our souls met
and exchanged an undying promise to each
other: "i vow to love you through each
blinding year i am away, relentlessly trying to
get back my other half." after all of it was said,
one soul looked to the other and spoke of a tale
that had once been shared amongst the others:
"there is a secret between this world and the one
of which has yet to form that once we are separated
during the chaos, it will always take more than just
love for us to be together again. heartaches and
broken dreams. distance between good mornings
and heartbeats. saying a final goodbye to the one
you thought was forever, but realizing forever was
never intended to last that long. this is what brings
us together in the end. the ones who are meant to
be. tragedy and bliss will always lead you to that
unexpected kiss. until then, never give up searching.
we do not get to decide how long we are here.
we wear the number on our backs and only those
who know this secret, can be reunited again. live a
life where being afraid of not finding the one only
strengthens your belief in love."

and i will paint you a beautiful
picture with the ashes of the old
me. i keep them in a glass box
above my heart, acting like a
trophy. i know if i survived
those years, today will never
defeat this veteran's soul.

sometimes i absolutely hate myself for caring so much for others who do not give a shit about me. but i am this person for a reason and i do not hold grudges, nor will i ever. it is just nice to hear, "thank you or i am doing alright, thank you for asking." we are all made for a reason and if i have to search the corners of the universe to understand my presence or the lack there of, then i will. life is not about pleasing or accommodating others. it is about being happy with yourself and being able to put a smile on when all you have left to do is wipe tears from your face. each one that leaves you, is a piece of your soul that you will never get back again. remember that and the ones you give away on purpose or by accident. but if you need to, let them fucking fall like rain and kiss the ground. i know it has been difficult for you. i walk in mud daily because of mine.

when you look into my eyes, please see past the universe you think exists in me. i need you to realize that without you seeing a life together, my sky would fall and surround me with the darkness of the space that resides in my soul. without you, i am nothing more than a single particle of love, urgently searching for a heart that would love nothing more than to accept it as their own.

words cannot describe what it means
to be needed and not just wanted.
the difference in the two is simple:
if you want something, you can find
it anywhere. if you need something,
you only have to look to one place
and it will look as familiar to you as
the sun kissing the moon before the
universe awakes you to another
unification of miracles.

somewhere between the beat of the moon and stars, lies the truth of who we are. you will come to understand that our bodies are not ours. that our spirit is merely using us to guide it back to the home it was taken away from.

never allow another human to price your self-worth.

this is your life. fucking live it without unnecessary

apologies or unwanted goodbyes.

the humans that are not happy for your accomplishments or success, are the ones that no longer need to be around you for your journey. they are only in the backseat because you know they could never lead you where you needed but you enjoyed their company until today.

everybody likes you until success becomes your first and last name. some will leave and those that have been there, will always stay beside you. never allow your head to become bigger than your heart.

she did not have the passion to fit in or be of the   normal type. her fire was out of control, aiming to be the crazy and wild kind. all i could do was stand back with my eyes locked with hers, hoping our flames could dance all over the moon. together, we created a life that would burn in any world.

my life is complicated;

    like chaos meeting
    love for the first time.

    <my doubts remain fictitious>

maybe i am not anybody important to you, but to me, i am somebody. i am my very own hopes and dreams. i have been shaped and molded from an old soul to live in a world where humans are categorized by race, wealth, and titles. i am tired of all the bullshit that is going on around us. at night i turn to the moon and she even cries for the lost ones like me. those who have been to the depths of near death and slowly climbed back to life. with each breath i take, i try and inhale all of the negativity surrounding me and exhale my heart to those who need it. oftentimes, even it is not wanted, i have to keep reminding myself that better days are coming. you have to believe that. no matter your circumstance. money will never buy you a life worth a damn if you are not satisfied with who you are and where you come from.

there she was, holding her head as high as a human possibly could. she always loved to smell the fresh bloom of an early morning. it was as if she came to earth in order to love and appreciate a life so many take for granted. somehow, i managed to fall into her atmosphere just in time for her to save mine. she was such an infectious spirit and to know i was the one chosen to be there when she woke up, made me believe that heaven was always a dream that she brought to reality. a dream where her insatiable eyes were the sky that i wished would fall all over me, time and time again.

she wanted everything that life had ever taken away from her. so she fucking took it without permission. she grew tired of humans taking what they wanted without asking. if you are not willing to stand up for yourself, there is nothing off limits. her love for life was stronger than those who tried to tie her down with the chains that she once wore. she was born again and now lives in the wide open spaces between the sun and the moon; creating a new home for her hopes and dreams. reminding us all that if you are willing to fight for your freedom, death will just be a word that mortals are afraid to approach.

without beautiful souls like yours, i would just be another forgotten voice in a crowded room, whose echo becomes distorted and out of place. where shadows become a taunting menace that never leave you.

sometimes i feel like i will never get a chance to love you. and then i think what's the point of loving someone at all? it is a hard concept to grasp, but when you have half of a heart left, you must not love someone with it. be there for yourself and never forget that love will find us before we find it. after all, hearts are not meant to be played with, they are only meant to be held the most lovable ways.

i am no different than you. though you keep telling me that i have three eyes, while you only have two. i am this way for a reason and i accept who i am. my life is for me and i will always feel sorry for you. you have no idea the shit that i have been through, yet you stand amongst your group and ostracize a human who does not fit into what you call normal. i will never change my standards or adjust to your views. i am me, and that will always be enough for those who see the world as i do. i was not meant to be perfect. i was not made to be the same. we are all just lost souls with a face and different name. continue to mock me and call me those things, but i will keep walking by without ever giving into your ignorant and infantile ways. one day, we will all meet again and you will not have all of your friends. for you will be all alone, burning from the inside out. i might laugh a little, but i will never put you out or put you down the way you have abused me for the past ten years.

i am different, but we are all the same. you just hide your insecurities better.
<self-talks>

it was in her eyes that i finally found where the universe was created. when her eyes met mine, a new horizon was made. the one where i knew that my heart would be forever full and continue to rise and fall with each loving breath she took while saying my name. love me without boundaries. hold me without letting go. kiss me so we can both breathe together. that's the life i need and am dying for. so fucking love me for everything i know we can be together. let's be forever and burn the skies, lighting up the world for the universe to see what a twin flame looks like.

i am sorry for keeping you from
your dreams. but you once made
me think that i was the one.

now i am here, holding what is left
of my broken soul and trying to make
the pieces fit. for some reason these
shards of me will not go back together.

i guess they don't understand how to
mend and begin the process of moving
forward, when you have the key to my
salvation.

being in love means falling in love every day for the rest of your life. fall hard with each other and do not apologize to the onlookers who are of the jealous type. for they are the ones who once told you, "it will never work." continue to walk by, staring at love itself. a love they all tripped over with their tongues crawling out of their mouths and fell for with their own cowardly ways. if you are willing to never let go of each other's hand when life is desperately trying to rip you apart, being whole will be the most beautiful sensation you will ever feel.

and if it is love you want,
make sure your soul is
ready to help out when
your heart becomes too
full.

i want to know more about you. like how you fill your bountiful lungs with so much love and breathe it all into me. like how the angelic sound of your voice carries not only my name, but it makes me forget about my buried childhood pain. like how your delicate body is a temple of lost art that only i have discovered. my mind gets so heavy at night with thoughts of you, my knees become my feet as i pray to the heavens for allowing me to be with you. i want to know where a lovely human like you came from and go back there together as one. you have fed my soul all of the passion it will ever need. so please, my light, tell me more about where you came from.

love is more than just saying, "i do."
love is about the 3am conversations
where neither one of you wants to
stop talking. where a dinner and a
movie means watching the moon
and stars, while devouring each
other's thoughts. how a slight touch
of one's hand can take you back in
time when it was love at first sight.
love is about a never-ending dance,
involving two partners that are madly
in love with just the chance of falling
in love every day for the rest of their lives.

some of the surest bets i have
made in my life, are the ones
i've had to double down on.
i have never broken even, but
i am learning how to hold a
hand i never want to fold.

she is the most wild and magical flower of love i have ever held in my hands. for the rest of my life, i will constantly breathe her in; getting high off of her soul and lost in her heart.

an older lady was standing in front of my girlfriend and i, wearing a blue evening dress and a daisy placed in her hair. i guess she had got it done earlier that day. you could notice how it stayed in place as the wind blew through us. she was by herself and i wanted to ask if she was waiting on someone, but as soon as i could open my mouth, another woman approached her. "mom. where did you go?" the little ole lady turned around and smiled. "i have been waiting on you dear. i told you before we left that i wanted to ride it one last time." her daughter asked if they could go ahead of us. you see, the lady was not in line for the ride. she was off to the side, looking up with her eyes locked to the sky. i had overheard her earlier talking out loud, "where the hell did all of my time go? i should have said something, but i didn't want to interrupt her moment. all i said was, "yes mam. we don't mind at all. enjoy the night." the lady thanked me and started crying. i knew it was something special when the tears fell on my shoulder. she hugged me out of nowhere and i smiled as if i had just saved the world or something. "when i was younger, your age probably, i fell in love at the fair. my late husband asked me if i wanted to ride the ferris wheel and i told him no because i was afraid of heights. so this will be my first time riding one." i told her, "have fun and savor every minute the world stops spinning for us and starts rotating for you." she smiled at me and thanked me again. every time we go back there, i think of the little ole lady who made the world become hers, while making a memory that lasted a lifetime for us. we have been together ever since that night and today will mark fifty years. you will never know when or where they come from, but some of those that we call human, are actually much more than that. they are teachers of life.

<a short story>

back before i became me, i was you. searching the abyss of what was my mind. drowning in yesterday's thoughts and trying to give old memories the breath i thought they needed. turns out i was not only swimming with my hands and feet tied together, i was keeping my past alive. i managed to break free of those ropes that had almost killed me and arrived at the gates of a new future. one where the possibility of life became my goal, as well as to reach out to those who were being weighed down by an endless amount of lost hope. i have come to realize over the years that life is an exact metaphor for surviving. where every day could be our last, yet we fight like hell to keep moving forward, kicking and screaming if we have to. whatever you have to do, break free of the negativity that embodies you. your soul will thank you later. we are all born to do extraordinary things. believe that and you will figure out life. the fight always starts and ends on the inside.

i was once told, "do not ever give your heart to anyone, because they will always drop it." sometimes we drop our own hearts and it is our fault, yet nobody likes to take the blame. especially when it is self-inflicted. i am man enough to understand that this was all because of me. i do not need to hear another apology. i just need to live life for me right now.

life is full of illusions. you have to learn
to see past the universe for what it is.
look deeper and understand that
everything is created to die.

death is for certain, but we all choose how
to live. live loudly and be contagious with it.
death might take me sooner rather than later,
but i will throw stars at those who never had
a wish come true. i am willing to give my all
to make others happy and to feel alive.

i hope one day that a smile can cure any illness.
i can only hope that my touch can cure the ache
that plagues you tonight. do not destroy beautiful
things in order to get what you want.

sometimes, the things you mistake to be for forever,
tend to be the tragic ending of it all. but even with
that, a beautiful detour to your opening act could
be a few seconds away.

i once sat with my tired mind resting in the depths of my hands, contemplating the life that was in front of me. it was hard to see, because i was too damn young and naive to appreciate the finite details around me. when i was a teenager, i often caught myself looking at a round world through square eyes. i had to do a lot of soul searching over the years, but i finally came to an abrupt conclusion: in order to appreciate everything the universe has given to me, i would eventually need to adapt and mold my eyes by using the sights and sounds of both the sea and land. to become one with the people around me was crucial in developing my soul. to know who you are, you must first understand those who walk amongst you; aimlessly or with a purpose. we are all clowns and puppets, roaming the earth, looking for our right kind of circus. until then, i will laugh with you and together we will create such an event that everyone will see past their square eyes and start living beyond the realms of their own forgotten imagination.

life is the only constant change we face. instead of fighting the idea, learn to embrace it and your life will begin to not only make sense, but a purpose will be born from it. do not put restraints on something that is meant to roam wildly amongst mortals.

just like lightning striking the sand on the lonely beaches at night, the right kind of energy will create the most pristine objects humans have ever seen. we will be forged for life. we will watch the colors and become the brilliance that flows between the moon and her heartbeats.

until you have been broken, do not come talk to me.
we already have nothing in common. i still have shards
from my nightmares stuck in my throat, trying to cut
their way out. it isn't that i don't have anything to say.
i just rather be in pain while talking about beauty and
depths, instead of the smallest of all talks.

life is such an agonizing and spirit wrenching place at times. hell, even love teases you with the possibility of forever. but i will continue to swim against the current until there is no more water to tread. with our naked hearts and jubilant souls, we will never again be divided by two sides of the sea. one day, the waves of hope will finally rest on the shorelines of love. that, my dear, is a promise i will die trying to keep.

i am merely the mirror image of what my soul
tries to portray through words. the struggle.
the pain. the heartache. the love i keep inside.
this is me. this is how the sun rises again and
keeps me alive for the night.

i once went to this AA meeting and the room was
full of these beautiful souls who got lost between
finding themselves and reaching for another drink
or getting their needle ready for the morning hit.
i listened to the stories and i thought to myself,
"my god, the entire world is here in front of me."
for that moment in time, i was right where i
needed to be. understanding struggle is more
than just not having a meal. it is comprehending
the fact that we are all fucked up in our own crazy
ways. to be in a room filled with people actually
trying to save themselves and knowing there are
millions of people addicted to a false truth, it puts
depression into my heart. but i cannot save you this
time. it is your fight and warriors travel thousands of
miles by foot or mind to defeat what is before them.
life is not living unless you are trying to make a
difference for yourself and others. if you think i
am lying, i will save you a seat at the next meeting.

the sun has always reminded me that

no matter how much rain one soul has

felt and seen, it will always be able to

dry off and comfort those in need.

i know i do not have the perfect smile. i understand i have never had the perfect past. for i am a sinner and i am not ashamed of the things i have done. i am here now, and i am perfect for the ones who never left. because of that, my definition of perfect will never be like yours. so judge me and smother me with your callous words, but i will always have a life worth meaning even if you cannot read the writings i've painted throughout the walls of my life. i love who i am and where i am going is still unknown right now. i am still walking, breathing, and burning my own path to find the hope i need. i am not perfect, hell, nothing about me is. an imperfect soul is an incredible human once you get to know them. here i stand though, still trying to be as imperfect as i can. never allowing myself to fit into what society deems as the proper way to live because that is being normal. now why would anyone want to be that?

it's as if you forgot everything you learned and just lost your goddamn mind to the wild riches inside your body. you taught yourself how to forgive by letting go of the blame, but now you don't know how to function without it. losing who you are is a terrible disease and most never make it back to who they were. it becomes easier once you sit down the mountains you have been carrying and appreciate the journey each one revealed to you.

strangers have been the backbone of who i am.
maybe we are too strange for ourselves and
welcome anything resembling what it is
we are longing for. maybe we are the
occupants of another world, but got
lost along the way.

being myself has always been a challenge.
i have feelings rushing over me each time
i am around a crowd or negative energy.
the meaning behind it, is force meeting
peace. it is our choice which we love and
neglect. it is our choice which we feed
and starve that allows our lives to expand
into something more than just bones and
regrets.

we were so close to magic, but settled for the dust it leaves behind when it goes looking for a different love. there is no replacing a spirit who was always there for you, but you can become something greater for yourself if you wish to take on the feelings trading turns trying to change your ' softness. battling for your sanity is the only option left when everything else leaves.

you cannot help those who wish to cause pain and try to end whatever life you thought you had before them. all you can do is take your reasons with you and remove yourself from the situation. you will make it. you will make it. you will make it. be yours before anyone else's. be yours before attempting to be something else for someone who has never gotten to know their own struggles.

as the rain fell quietly last night, i looked over and caught a glimpse of your face. funny how certain things remind us of those who no longer share the same space. as a kid, when the storms approached my house, i felt like i was never close enough to its magic. the same feeling invited itself back into my room disguised as a memory of you.

finding a chance to be closer to your warmth, i slip into
the night with you underneath me, softly pressed against
my body, moving with the sky above us. never out of turn
or reasons to make the other wildly moan.

<we are the animals clawing their way out of their own sin>

i will never be able to say hello again and think i can survive the goodbye after losing the world that was next to me. some goodbyes completely annihilate your foundation and rearrange your heart and mind.

your apology only made me realize how much more i deserved. i give too much of myself for the scraps others leave behind. i have to be better at feeding myself and not giving out pieces hoping to catch someone who in the end only wanted to feel loved rather than to be loved. i know the difference now.

if you are seeking closure, it is unnecessary.
i have had my chest ripped open for years
without any sense of healing, but i found
out love was hiding where they could never
see me. i am my own reset. i control it all.

if you need to cry, open yourself up to it. if you need to run, let go of your fears. if you need to live, you must resist the safety and jump. you must do this in order to feel something for someone again. maybe you aren't looking for anything resembling that all, but you should at least want to have it for yourself. if you don't, no one will ever be there long enough to try.

the universe in you aligned with the one in me. never has the sky looked as open as it does tonight. it is surreal what can happen when you focus your energy on people who actually care about the stars as much as some care about finding someone to share them with.

if i could ask anything from you, just hold me while
i find the strength to go on and find my way back to
this life. i never left you. i have always been lost.

/forgive me for losing sight of the
face that stared too long at the sun\

i don't know how to do anything
but feel. the past. the present.
the future. they are all after what
i cannot give. i am a prisoner to
the calling. i am a free man to the
cause. i am fighting a battle i have
bled for before. though the hurt,
that goddamn hurt, it still shows
me how to live again and
rebel against it all.

you will never escape what is meant for you until it reveals the reasons why it is here. patience is a token we don't always take, but need to learn how to hold without using it on the wrong things.

i thought i had waited too long
to move on from where i was.
the roots took to me and forced
my hands to cut myself away
from you. it has been the
greatest lesson in healing
and how sometimes we are
in denial about the love we
have for someone who cannot
see it for themselves.

take a look at your life and appreciate those who left. we are continuous in motion, but not everything in it stays after we stop.

all of my life i have been reckless and young.
my age never caught up with me and my
mind resisted anything close to safety.
i built the walls and kept the night to
myself. we are all devils and angels
living in bodies made to look like
humans free of sin.

you made me believe in my brokenness and turned it
into something worth keeping. something entirely
made from soul. something not everyone will
understand. something that keeps me safe
and reluctant to second guess my next move.

i want you to wear nothing and allow me
to love you in your vulnerability. leave your
eyes open. keep your hands still and above
your head. my mouth will call to your lips,
but stay patient. my hands will lower and
raise you gently, but stay patient. i am going
to go nice and slow, marking you and making
you mine. tenderly and patiently following
your movements, i will teach you how to
listen to me without uttering a single word.
before we are done tonight, we will become
entangled in the raw nature of obedience
and stimulation encompassing the mind,
body, and spirit.

until you have felt love leave you, you will
never understand what death for the living
can feel like. being ruined is the cost of
saying yes to tomorrow, but it's the
rush to feel again that keeps us
alive.

a world without you is a place i never want to be a part of. you are the reason my universe still holds both the sun and moon. losing you means being left in the dark when the light has retreated underneath the sky. i would have zero energy to pull back the stars and find it. if you should leave, all of my limbs would fall off, leaving a motionless and disturbed creature for anyone else looking to find me.

dance, sweet woman.

        show me how you want to be held.
        it will be the last time you will ever
        have to guide my hands to where
        you need them. muscle memory is
        a wild thing once you learn the
        sensitive parts of the soul.

if you are to ever fall in love,
fall for the one who teaches
you how to be in love with
yourself first before stepping
off the edge of the world
where you may or may not
make it back alive.

from that point forward, i learned
how words can fill a heart and kill
it at the same time.

<the lies we sleep with>

sometimes, goodbyes are excuses we

forget to say in the beginning to

keep someone from finding out the

truth of who we are.

according to some, you have died already and are lifeless. you don't have to prove anyone wrong. you just have to be able to walk and breathe and laugh again. you will make it there. if i can crawl out of my own grave, so can you. the first handful of earth brings the bravery you need to fight for the second one.

if you kiss me, i cannot promise you the next fifty years. i can only guarantee to never let go of this moment and to live for more filled with you being the cornerstone of what i wish to build.

you and i share the same sun.
for us, we will never be in the
dark.

with a connection like this,
flesh only gets in the way.

maybe we never had a fucking a chance at surviving this. maybe that's how it's supposed to be. maybe we are perfect for each other, but not for this world.

when your eyes found mine,

it was the first time i had ever

been sure about anything

in my life.

keeping it together has never been my thing.
i am a crazy mess occupied with wise tales
and oceans not meant for anyone to
swim in. most of the time i stand on the
shore and think who else in this universe
looks around and sees only themselves.
sometimes i wonder if the feeling of being
alone means being able to love yourself
without needing anyone to confirm what
you already know. my mind fucks me
more than life itself, but it keeps me
safe from listening to the lies others
die from.

the moon never forgets those who dance devilishly under her light. there you will find truth. there you will come to know what kind of human you are. there you will find out how love can destroy you in the most wildest of ways.

thank you for showing me what love never could be, so i could teach myself what love actually is. lessons are only that if you wish to learn from your mistakes and past transgressions. a child will know love before you because he or she already knows the proper way to be themselves without having to prove anything to anyone. and that alone is a gift most of us end up without as we get older. maybe the child dies in us all after so long, but we neglect the truth so we can attain some sense of the word for our own fulfillment, rather it works out or not.

what we are doing has never been done before. there are no rules as to how it is intended to work. we can only hope we do what is necessary for us to live and love as if we have it figured out. trial by fire is the logic we are using, and may we fucking burn with the sun.

you might not to be who you thought you'd be five, ten, or twenty years ago. you must not let that keep you from pursuing who you can be right now. where you are and where you want to be is all about what you are willing to do to change it if you want. he heart will never give up on a dream as long as you feed it confidence.

she loves hearing coca-cola fizzing, the smell of fresh cut grass, and the sensation of the ocean's air against her face. forehead kisses provide her comfort and being snuggled allows her to let go of the day. lay down a blanket under her favorite tree and watch how the world spins for her. we are the kind of love that gives their all for the cosmos in order for the universe to never feel left out.

if i stay too long in one place, something inside of me dies. something i can never afford to lose. my energy is best served while adventuring from one idea to the next, only stopping to say hello and thank you.

we are who we are, because all of our lives, we have always been who we needed to be for the one we were with.

we adapt for the betterment of not only us, but for the world when it gets dark during the day.

<empath>

the night our souls held
each other tight;

    forgetting humans even existed.

        /light-lovers\

i tried to figure out a way to tell you how much i love you. so i decided to tell the whole world instead. it made sense because you are my world. you are my true love and soul mate. together we will explore the galaxies of fate and teach them how love conquers all.

(l)iving

(o)ur

(v)ows

(e)very day

she was the type of girl that could laugh at herself, even when life tried to get the best of her. she knew that she was stronger than any of the bullshit trying to knock her down. she was determined to live her life, not through the acceptance of others, but through her own understanding that she was in fact capable of loving herself more than the judgment of her company. for she always knew that no matter what happened, she would always stay true to who she was before falling victim to the opinions of those humans that were below her.

i told her,

"i am ready to be scared. i need to feel what it's like to touch you and fear what it would be like to lose you. i am ready to live. i need to experience what being alive feels like while our bodies are entangled between the sheets of our dreams and desires. i am finally ready to open my heart and allow you to see what i've been holding back from others. the love that resides in it has always been too much, always too strong for those who were scared to feel it. i want my hands to only hold yours and i need my eyes to see you every waking day and every sleepless night. i am finally ready to give you what i have never shared with anyone before you; my life. my soul. my promises. everything down to the broken pieces of my heart i've kept in my pockets, strenuously trying to put together myself. when i am with you, i am ready for it all; the sensual pain. the overwhelming happiness. the nervous sensation in my bones i get from your fingertips walking down the spine of my back. holding you, i am willing to love and cherish every naked inch of you, beginning now and beyond the last breath we share together."

give a human rules and you will
see the lines start to grow.

allow a human a choice and you
will see the world begin to bloom.

as her fingernails were digging deeper into the back of my soul, i saw her mouth open as she began to moan. setting off every fiber in my body to pin her against the earth and allow her see what it is like making love to someone who wants nothing more than to please the one they are with.

life will forever give you certain things
to better your chances, but it will also
take away from you as well. we might
never totally understand why or the
reasoning behind it, but at this point
in my life, i am grateful for 2am
conversations and 3am honesty.
people often wonder how one
becomes an insomniac and this
is what i live for. no matter how
much rest i do or do not get, i am
waiting for another sleepless night
to learn you and what it is you crave
when sleep escapes us both.

the greatest thing i've ever shared
was a smile. whether it be with
the broken ones who never had
a chance at life or with the ones
who thought they were complete
by being better than me.

always remember what a new day
could mean for somebody. it might
be the first time they get to share
anything with someone who
believed in the power of taking
time to appreciate their life.
no matter who they are.

there are days when i get tired
of life and i just want to be;

>
> *to be loved.*
> *to be at peace.*
> *to be with you.*

it was always the little things that made
us fall for each other every single day.
we never complicated life because we
knew how it could mess up everything
we worked so damn hard for.

    even if it was our worst day,
    all we needed to hear was,
        "i love you."
    it's the little things in life
    that give life meaning.

the love you know is the love that will never leave you. no matter how many times you leave yourself, it will be there time and time again. it knows how to heal and how to give you space when you need it. it knows you, **because a soul never forgets a body who loved it, too.**

standing here with a wild heart in my

hands, i am afraid of what it wants

and i am terrified why it beats madly

for things i cannot have.

you've always been the love you needed.
it doesn't matter if your mother left you.
it doesn't matter if your father ran away.
it doesn't matter if you are lost in this
fucking rabbit hole. the tears mean you
care, and that's why you will make it.
don't become numb like those who
show nothing but hatred and resent.
be your own kind of determination.
be the reason instead of an excuse.

i am foreign to this body.
i am lost to this feeling.
i am confused by humans
who can't appreciate the
sky. i am not made for this
place. i am not made to be
here. i missed my landing
spot and now i am suffering
to be somewhere i am not
sure even exists, but i know
it calls out to me in the
moments i feel alone.

we were both completely broken, and to us, it was a beautiful thing. we allowed each other to heal properly, without saying anything. our eyes made for conversation and our hands provided the remedy. a love so pure and genuine, together, we found speaking with our hands made for a better conversation.

the origin of who you are is tied to the
destiny dancing around your desires.

> *keep dancing, moon child.*
> *keep singing, unearthly human.*
> *keep loving, sweet evergreen.*

give me your hand and i will place a single star in it for you

to place anywhere in the sky. that is our point. that is ours

to sleep under and love for the rest of our breaths.

being a traveler means constantly
picking up your soul to discover
what's underneath it. the roaming
it endures leads to the kind of
beauty poets fall in love with.

relying on someone for your

own happiness is handing

over a loaded gun. only one

survives and gets to tell their

story of how it was self-defense.

scars do not dictate who we are.
they are simply storyboards as to
how we came to be the wonderful
and chaotic versions of a human
not quite sure of its purpose or
balance.

do not apologize for the wolf inside of you.
sometimes we just have to let go and
release it back into the wild where
we were meant to be.

all the devils and angels cast out before my
time, live within me.
i am made of their sins and apologies.
i reside in the truth my voice breaks against.

i fear my heart will never stop beating for the madness
and i'll run around like a dog chasing car tires looking for
the perfect words to say and not fucking it up or succumbing
to the vehicle of life.

picket signs and picking sides. homeless lines longer than what the shelters can provide. an economy that is ran by crooked fakes and lying eyes. how does the world keep so much inside? the universe must be laughing at us all, talking amongst themselves, "these humans still haven't learned a damn thing. what small lives they live, trying to survive while they continue to murder their own kind." this world is not powered by the money or officials. it is powered by soulless humans and their lonely agendas.

i believe in this world we all have music as a common denominator. where we all can relate, because music is a part of us. with each beat that is played, it touches our souls and makes them dance. it is the lifeblood and we are all universal donors.

in life, chaos is all around us. it's only then do we appreciate the silence we oftentimes take for granted. do not get lost in the noise that embodies other humans. if you allow your soul to guide your words and actions,, there will always be peace within your heart. once we come to understand this feature of life, the world as we know it will change for the better. remember, it takes being broken into a million fucking pieces to truly find the identity of who we are. more often than not, those shards of life will ultimately form into a guiding light for those who are lost amongst the scattered particles of the sky.

i can taste your tears in the rain as the clouds cry from all of earth's pain. your eyes used to cry the same way from all the misery and heartbreak. you keep blaming yourself as if it was your mistake. but rest assured, i will take all of the blame. i never meant to cause you so much suffering. all i wanted to do was love you. when it is all said and done, i broke the one heart i cared for more than my own. all because i thought your needed a better home.

i woke up this morning to a sky as curious as your eyes. i then rolled over and kissed your forehead, whispering into your ear, "thank you for never leaving me." as i walked outside with my tea, i looked up and said, "thank you for the angel you sent to save me. she is asleep right now, but she is more than just alive inside. she is the gift i am allowed to open every day i get another chance at trying to make sense of this life."

i fell in love with her, but more importantly, i fell in love with who she wanted to be. it takes strength and courage to seize your dreams, while living in a world dominated by people who constantly search for normalcy. and my god, did she ever want more than just to walk through life being normal. she wanted all that life had to offer and then some. she wanted the whole goddamn thing. no matter what happened, i was going to support her because she never gave up on me. in her eyes, if she was not striving to become the person she was destined to be, she would forever live out her dreams in her sleep.

a little girl, probably no older than eight, sits on the sidewalk every single day. she draws with her chalk images i have never seen before. along side those are words that a young child should not know. she drew a peace symbol and wrote underneath it, "hope sits patiently and waits for humans to open their eyes. hoping they see life is more than just about dollar signs." above that was a drawing of a heart, outlined in the words, "love is cruel, though without it, there is no you and i." i honestly could not believe my eyes when she showed me what she called her masterpiece. i asked her, "where did these words come from, child?" she giggled like all little girls do, and said, "my soul."

the stars would not just fall, but they would land softly in our wild hearts. the universe created time and space in order for us to meet in this exact place. there was never enough light for me to love someone the right way until now. the distance that was dividing us was the fault line needed for the world to create the mountains we now stand on in the sky. from here on out, i will have the most beautiful view. i will always hold you above me, in every aspect of life. together we will forget what breathing alone feels like.

even if i had given her my whole heart, i knew my soul would never be enough. a deafening silence filled my lungs as she left with my last breath of love. in the end, all she wanted were diamonds, but all i could afford were the stars. looking up at them now, i still admire their beauty and how priceless they really are.

deserving to be full on everything mad and strange around me, i will throw up my bones to make more room for the things i enjoy and the people i love. life is too short to be starving yourself on yesterday. your hindsight needs to become the reason why you have made a change. if that offers you an alternative to the pursuit of what you are after, venture towards it and feed your soul while you still can. anything less than that and you are cheating the progress you have made. each step is a chance, a sacred opportunity to grow exponentially with who you have been running from when they said, "you'll never make it," and you believed those words. i have learned by altering my thoughts that you are in fact capable of loving the nothingness you thought you were made out to be.

i will never get tired of loving you and trying to make you smile. it is not only my life i want you to be in, i want to be in yours as much as you will have me. your presence is only comparable to the stars floating above us, wholesome and calm, they ask nothing, but only show us how to keep shining long after we are gone. there is a bravery inside of you that i desperately want you to see. i will continue breaking my dreams into halves for you to have at least a piece of the only thing i can give to you now.

keep yourself occupied with trying to be better. with trying to understand yourself more. with listening to your intuition and not looking for acceptance. you will never find that amongst these humans. you are too new and strange to them. keep yourself upright and walking towards the next adventure you seek.

there are still moments i see you as you were before they changed you. it is how i will always remember you. it is how the sun will breathe your name. it is how the moon will embrace your flaws and show you hers to let you know even through darkness and light, we are not even a portion of who we really are. you will always be the girl who smiles at random times during the day to ensure your mind that everything will be okay.

i am not for everyone and that is what i am most proud of. being this way is all it takes for me to envision my next step, my next thousand miles of endless thoughts and unforgettable love with everything around me that calls out to me. i listen to it all and feel it all, all the time. i used to think it was a curse, but once you tap into the soul of where you are, everything comes up loving you more. even the dead reach up from their graves to greet you and thank you for noticing beauty others always walk past.

i constantly wonder;
wandering around
my own mind.
aimlessly attempting
to create words to
relate the feeling
you get when love
tries to bury you
alive with words
you cannot describe.

for i am not trying to win your heart.
i am trying to understand your soul.
for a soul's recognition and acceptance
of it's other half is worth more.

<twin souls>

through the chaos erupting around
me, i stay as calm as the quiet sea.
not knowing what lurks at the bottom
is still an unknown mystery. push me
hard enough and i will take you to the
bottom of that quiet sea. there you
will see what chaotic company
encompasses me.

trying to hide and evade the
noose that almost strangled
you. the rope wasn't long
enough and you managed to
elude the pain and reality;
the struggle with love. it pulls
you like a tug of war, in which
your soul is trying to give more
than what your heart is fighting for.

you see, when i took the vow to always
be there for you and never leave, i loved
you the only way i knew how; until death.
i promised you this and i hope you do not
shed a single tear right now after our final
kiss. where i am going, the memory of you
will reside in my soul and keep me safe
until we meet again. whenever you feel like
missing me is too much for you, just know
that i will be watching you from the clouds
smiling, as i am telling stories about how i
am waiting on my angel. never forget what
i whispered in your ear our first night together,

"i will wait forever."

when she would walk,

the clouds would fight

amongst each other,

in hopes of being her

final step home.

you can be mad at me tomorrow, but
don't be mad at me today. you did this
to yourself. i never asked you to change.
i just told you there was a better way.
but you kept pushing yourself closer
to the edge. instead of reaching for
my hand, you reached for the ledge.
the thought of struggling for just one
more day was too much to bare, but
you did it your way. now all i ask is
for you to trust me and take my hand.
together we will solve this and build
a new plan. i love you more than life
itself. can't you see that in the end
it is about letting go your past and
reaching for a future filled with
possibilities. so let's go home
and step away from the edge.
i love you too much to see you
do this again.

/self-talk\

in the stillness of the night is when i search
to find the light illuminating from your eyes;
attracting my soul to venture off into the dark,
vetting for love. i shall find them, and when i do,
i will tell them hello and how much i have missed
seeing you.

/when the lights go out\

in her mind, she was a fucking legend.
i made it a point to test that theory
out one night.

as my soul melted into her eyes,
my body stayed behind, trying
to find a love that was lost
somewhere in the sheets.

she was not just a legend, but a
reality where truth actually speaks.

i will never forget those who have helped me to get where i am at today. for it is just a small step, but it is a step i thought i would never be able to take. no matter how big or small it is, forward motion is the key. just remember that no matter where this life takes you, direction is not the goal. it can mislead you at times and make you think you are going somewhere you want to go. life is about going where you need to go. never follow others to get where you are born to live.

if i wait for you, will you stand in the rain with me
and drink the dreams coming down from the heavens?
getting drunk on promises and the understanding that
love is nothing more than waiting a lifetime to die with
your soulmate; only to become born again in the next
life. wait with me and i swear i will be in your arms
forever. making love to every inch of your naked
emotions and hidden secrets that we will share
together. wait for me and i will never leave your
side. not even time will be able to tell us to leave
this world. we will forever be the makers and
keepers of what we have created.

please wait with with me, my love.

and if life should ever get in-between you and i,
i will attach our memories to my heart, with just
enough string and fly it in the sky for you to
always see; wherever i go, you will forever be
a part of me.

i will shed my soul to cover your
naked bones. you are not
different my love.

you are a gorgeous human and
you will never be alone.

this deranged world will not wreck
you, nor will it steal away a heart
that has always been my home.

that's why i am here. to love you
forever and protect you from it all.

some people say that i am too real, almost too good to be true. all i can tell you is, i am more soul than human. though i would like to expound on that subject more, i have almost died a thousand times, while others have barely lived their own bloody lives. they walk in the shadows of others, waiting for the sun to shine on them. i create my own sunlight and walk in the rays of hope every day my feet hit the floor.

for me, that is all i need and nothing more.

gripping your hands, i think i finally have a grip on reality. to me, drinking you in with every moment we spend talking about how the earth is not big enough for us, is exactly what i need. i blackout with your love. i forget a wretched place even exists in our universe. you curse under your breath, but you revel in what we have created.

/only love gets in\

i will spend my last days waiting

to kiss you once more. i know i

do not have much time left, so

the precious breaths i take, i will

save them for you, and only you.

as the last words fall slowly from

my lips, i hope they'll sink into

your beating heart and find a

place where we will never be apart.

as my dad was leaving yet again, i remember waving to him as he drove away from all of the madness. my life was far from perfect and i wanted to know where the universe had taken it. most of my friends were happy and enjoying life, all the while i sat behind chaos, not understanding why. then it dawned on me when i was thirteen that my life will always be like this, because i was destined to recall memories that have haunted me, so at night, when the world sleeps, the ghosts of my dreams do not go searching for another soul to take. i have sacrificed for the greater good. hopefully down the road, i will not be riding shotgun in this story that i wrote. maybe, just maybe, i will be able to ride beside a woman who loves me, instead of the turbulent times that i am currently lost in.

i remember this one time when i was younger, where there was a moment of clarity in my life that i witnessed through my kaleidoscope eyes. the world to me was a 3D image at such a young age. i saw colors dance off the sky and twirl in her hair. where we were together for a brief moment, then we too were evaporated to mist upon the summer's air. together, we experienced life and it was right then and there i understood love; for it was not in the moments we shared with each other, but in the years since we have been apart. love will never leave you no matter where you have gone. it resides in the breaths you take and the people you leave behind. love is constantly flowing through our souls and oftentimes dies within our bones. love to us was never about a word or a feeling. it was simply based off the understanding that when we were together, we were happy and happy is all we ever needed.

spread your wings child.

   let the world see what it is like to fly without the
help of those who have always tried to restrain
your beauty. fly for me and with me. let's soar
above the clouds of doubt and experience
heaven's gravity. allow for it to pull us in,
but never for it to capture our magic. what we
have is something that not even magic can touch.
our love is fucking bright and i love it too much
for others to copy. we are our own spell and i am
so in love with the way we fly together. as we go,
our feathers will be given to the other song birds
so they can sing, too.

no matter how many
breaths i take,

i will love you until
the last one.

love asks us for effort.
without it, we are
pretending to be
something we aren't.

will you stay with me? even when i am sick and wilting away? like the flower without the rain. like the star without eyes that gaze from down below. everything gets lonely when nobody watches them and eventually dies from within.

/universal caregiver\

to me, all the hope i need
lies within us holding hands.
it's how our souls know
when to awaken and
travel the universe;
hoping we never
let go. as long as i
have your hand in mine,
we will travel in time,
holding onto hope and
allowing our souls a
chance at love.

if you have dreams go after them.

stop chasing them only when night

comes and you fall asleep. for at one

point in our lives, we too were just dreams.

i want to make you believe that love
can exist. where two people can feel so
connected by just one kiss. where the
truth is always better then the lies.
where there is no such thing as goodbyes.
where the truth will sometimes hurt, but
how loving you makes the pain subside.
i want to make you believe that anything
and everything is possible, even when things
don't go right. if only i could show you exactly
how you made me believe these things with just
your smile. i know we could change the world
together. i know that we could conquer love,
once and for all.

these days, i don't have a lot of friends anymore.
i am not ashamed to say it. all i need in this life,
is pen and paper to get me through the night.
my thoughts keep me company when love
leaves me alone.

never let anything get in the way of what your soul breathes for. it is the flower that gives us life and without it, we are merely petals without color or purpose drifting along the streams where we forgot to inhale its love.

and there is still light to be
found once you step outside
of yourself long enough to
enjoy the imagination of the
energy around you.

and there we were, sitting with each other and taking in all that we hope to have one day. dream by dream, we inched closer to the lips of a new a day. we brought with us a renovated sun and moon to hang in our sky. it is where our wishes will grow up to become everlasting roses, blooming from our eyes.

grow, sweet magic, grow.

her bones tell of a magnificent story;
a longing to break for something
incredibly wild and rare.

a heart like that only beats for adventures.

at the end of the day, i can only hope my soul is worn out from the wandering and traveling. i can only hope it follows me to the end of it all. i can only hope magic is still discussed between my dreams and reality. i can only hope these bones become a home it can love and grow in. maybe my soul has a name, but i just call it wanderer. it is always close to me, but it knows nothing ever happens to those who stay in one spot for their entire lives. maybe it does for some, but what i am after, i've had to leave behind a lot of good people to pursue it. that's living to me. friends come and go, but they will never give you your time back when you are eighty and on a bed you will never get out of. a handful will know you, and i hope to have at least two left that understood that part of me.

pain showed me how beautiful it actually is to feel even if it stays persistent. sometimes, that is the only way to teach yourself how to become the same way for the things you cannot live without. those same things will be the reason why it will eventually go away and be replaced by the touch of someone who actually cares about what you are going through and will not let you continue being in that state of mind. life is full of these healers, these light magicians, who know a kind of life you have lived. they won't leave you. they will be your heart, and in return, you will ultimately become theirs.

there will always be someone you can never become, but i do hope you enjoy discovering this version of yourself for a little while longer before stepping out and shedding your skin for the next phase of this incredible adventure. there are times she isn't quite sure of who she wants to be. there are nights that will forever hold her emotions and how they continue changing the way she sees the world. she likes it that way. even more so with a cup of tea and her spirituality blossoming into a new moon. she may have lost faith before in the love, magic, and miracles this world presents to us, though sometimes it can be a bit stubborn with its feelings, there will be more of it to come and more of it that follows the heart of a wanderer. taming a wild creature is something that should never be tried, because once you do, you will understand the difference between her bark and bite. the sun still skips across her eyes like the stones she holds and wishes on at night. her energy is abundant and only reserved for those who value a heartfelt conversation and seeks out the stars hiding behind forgotten eyes. it does get lonely. it does begin to become a weary drive. it does begin to hurt a little more than it should when you are evolving into the human you were created to be. but she still loves and listens and feels every inch of the earth spinning underneath and around her. her wings make it easy to forget that walking was once desired by many, but now we look to the sky to find ourselves.

www.ingramcontent.com/pod-product-compliance
Lightning Source LLC
Chambersburg PA
CBHW021946290426
44108CB00012B/973